A Gift For: _____

From: _____

Published by Hallmark Gift Books,
a division of Hallmark Cards, Inc.,
Kansas City, MO 64141
Visit us on the Web at Hallmark.com.

Editorial Director: Delia Berrigan
Editor: Jared Smith
Art Director: Jan Mastin
Designer and Production Artist: Dan Horton

ISBN: 978-1-59530-563-3
BOK1219

Printed and bound in China
AUG12

Enjoying the art of Retirement

GRIN BIG!

AND ASK FOR THE

SENIOR DISCOUNT

BY MELVINA YOUNG

Hallmark
gift books

If you miss a sunrise,
catch a sunset.

Wear sweatpants
only if you plan to sweat.

Nap proudly!
The days of pretending
to be awake in meetings
are over.

Grow your hair long . . . wherever
it happens to be growing.

Surround yourself with what
you love most.

Appreciate the good
things in life.

When you feel like it,
do some of them.

Buy bubble wrap.
Pop. Repeat.

Get caught in the rain on purpose.

Look them right in the eye,
grin big, and ask for
the senior discount.

It's not the end of a career.
It's the beginning of an adventure.

It's okay to dance slow
to fast music.

Love your grandkids.
Then send them home.

Watch old movies.

Forget the mistakes of your youth.
Make new ones.

Cry at anything you want to.

There are more cookies in the world
than you could ever eat.

Still . . . try.

Smile because you're retired.
Laugh because your co-workers aren't.

When you think about
what's heading your way,
have faith that most of it
will be good.

THE FUTURE GOES WHEREVER
YOU *Drive* IT

It's not the journey . . . it's the number
of rest stops on the journey.

If God had meant
for us to work forever,
He wouldn't have
invented Florida.

Your first "Memo to Self": no more freakin' memos.

Don't just lie on the couch all day.
Lie on the couch and grin all day.

Even a rowboat can feel like a yacht
when you've earned it.

A life lived without fear
is a life lived in full.

When you give of your things,
you are appreciated.

When you give of yourself,
you are loved.

A life of leisure is not a life of laziness.
Unless that's what you're going for.

Smile, and the world smiles with you.
Grin big enough and they'll know
you're retired.

EXERCISE
Your Right To
SIT DOWN

Let go of office grudges.

Except for that one guy
who ate all the donuts.

That's unforgivable.

**Dress up, dress down,
dress optional.**

You've made a good living to make
a good life. Well done.

You're finally your own boss.

Now only your spouse
can tell you what to do.

The day starts when you
say it starts.

The "good old days" are now.

Set a curfew . . . and break it.

Give free advice
but don't wait for it to be taken.

Write love letters to your sweetheart.
Hand-deliver them.

Tell a good fishing story.

Why teach an old dog new tricks
when the old ones still work so well?

Feel free to act someone else's age.

Experience counts.
Know the value of your own wisdom.

Go where the grass is greener.
Literally.

Say "Yes!" to less stress.

Always remember why you
worked so hard in the first place:
so you could stop working.

Life will always come with challenges.

That's exactly what makes it worth living.

Be who you've always said you are.

Make your own decisions.
No five-hour meetings
required beforehand.

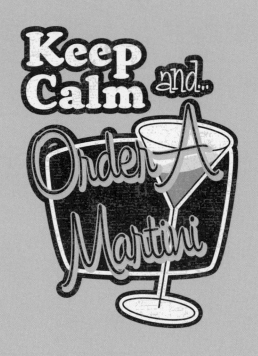

Keep Calm and... Order A Martini

There's no better time.

It's not just who you were.
It's who you have yet to become.

Keep the mind free,
and the body follows.

If a good book invites you in,
stay as long as you want.

Everywhere you go,
you take yourself.

Enjoy the company.

Meet new people.
Become friends with the ones you like.

Feel free to say "Good Morning"
in the afternoon.

Do something constructive . . .
just not today.

"Doing nothing" is hard work.
Be proud of your accomplishment.

Retirement isn't all
fun and games.

Sometimes it's paradise, too.

Live like a college kid again.

But with no parents
and much better beer.

Find places where you can be
shoeless, shirtless, and still get service.

Flirt a little.
Dance a lot.

A good camping spot
is wherever the RV stops.

See the world.

Even if it's from your flat-screen TV.

If you wake up feeling
like you should go back
to work . . . lie back down
until the feeling passes.

It's not *where* you are in life.
It's *what you do* with where you are.

Ponder the question of the cosmos:

Why do mattresses need tags
in the first place?

When one door closes . . . make
sure you lock it so you can
watch the TV in peace.

Cheese gets stronger with age.
Wine becomes more refined as it gets older.

There's a lesson in this somewhere.

**Think of all the time
you wasted as a kid.
There's finally time
to do it again.**

There are things
more important than money.

But they tend to cost money.

Work memories are fun *because* they're memories.

You are the discoverer of a whole new world.

You don't stop living just because you stop working for a living.

When you miss the hustle and bustle,
find new ways to hustle
and new places that bustle.

Now you can be paid in something
more important than money.

GENUINE   ORIGINAL

FIND A GYM
THERE'S USUALLY A
DONUT SHOP NEARBY

Go anywhere your mind will take you.
But no guilt trips.

You have a purpose-filled life.
You get to decide the purpose.

A new day calls for
new dreams.

When a 20-year-old gives you
unsolicited advice, try to be kind.

Even though you no longer have to.

No more fires to put out . . . unless
you build one first.

You don't have to clean up
anyone else's mess.

Unless you're married.

**Develop the fine art
of procrastination.**

Measure your life by laughter,
not by years.

Alarm clocks can only make
suggestions now.

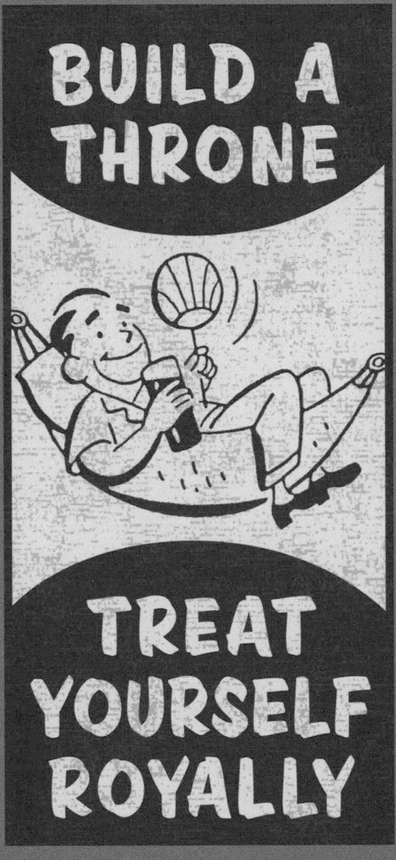
BUILD A THRONE
TREAT YOURSELF ROYALLY

Repeating yourself just proves
how reliable you are.

A big grin is the only face-lift you need.

Try to avoid stress.

If it can't be avoided,
try to hit it with your golf cart.

Whatever doesn't kill you . . . get
up and do again the next day.

Invite your grandkids over often.
It keeps the computer working.

Make a holiday last a "holi-week."

It's not that you're getting older.
It's just that younger people are
born every day.

Migrate. That's what free birds do.

It doesn't matter what you drive to the parade. It's the joining that counts.

One word that can
no longer strike fear
in your heart:

"meeting."

FINALLY, NOW YOU HAVE ENOUGH TIME TO FIGURE OUT JUST HOW MANY THINGS CAN BE FIXED WITH DUCT TAPE

You've invested responsibly . . .
in your kids,
your spouse,
your friends.

Now's the payout.

Why drive when you can walk?

Don't forget to be childish sometimes.

Ask yourself:

Is it worth living twice as long if you can't eat the full-fat ice cream?

When your mind plays tricks on you,
at least try to enjoy the show.

Try not to think about sex
all the time.

Some of that time
could be spent doing it.

Consider the move from
bifocals to trifocals
a promotion for your eyes.

Don't panic when you forget
your own phone number.

You rarely need to call yourself.

Learn a new language.
Or re-learn an old one.

Remember:
you can't drive with the top down
without getting a few bugs
in your teeth.

Go back to college.
Go to class this time.

There may be denial, anger,
bargaining, and depression . . . but
eventually your co-workers will
accept your retirement.

It's time to follow your dreams.

Hit the alarm and keep
right on following them.

Now whenever someone says
something dumb, you can laugh
on the outside, too.

Today is your day.

And so is tomorrow.

And the day after . . .

Who you are cannot be
summed up in what you did
for a living.

Take your time.
It's all yours.

HAVE YOUR NEST EGG
SUNNY-SIDE UP

The only people
you have to kiss up to
are the ones
you actually want to kiss.

Party like you don't have
to go to work tomorrow.

Nude beaches should be
experienced from inside the
comfort of swim trunks.

Dare to go places with
bad cell-phone reception.

Finally, your "To Do" list can become
your "Wanna Do" list.

Go crazy.

**Just not
"Let's get arrested!"
crazy.**

Don't try to keep up with trends.
They're just one more thing that
moves faster than you do.

Never be afraid to play
the AARP card.

RVs make excellent summer homes.
And winter homes.

Retirement isn't all hammocks
and sunny days.

It's rainy-day snoozing, too.

The weekend is now
every day.

If "even a little kid can do it,"
that explains why you can't.

You could write something down . . .
but then you'd have to remember
where you put the list.

Retirement paradox:

You'll have to buy
your own office supplies.

But you will no longer
need office supplies.

At 18 you gain your independence.

At retirement you finally
gain your freedom.

Who needs money when there's love?

The electric company doesn't count.

You're not getting old.

These are your "vintage" years.

Become the star
of your own reality show:

"The Biggest Snoozer."

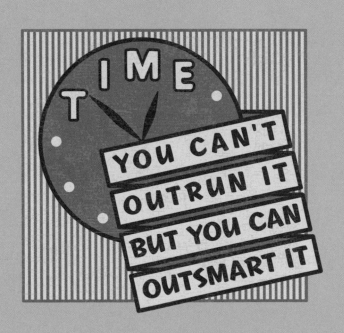

TIME

YOU CAN'T OUTRUN IT BUT YOU CAN OUTSMART IT

If time feels like it's speeding up,
it's because you're in
the driver's seat now.

You finally have time
to figure out what life's all about:

not having to figure anything out.

At the end of the day,
what really matters
is that you spent it
exactly how you wanted to.

Funny how when
you set your own hours,
there are never enough of them.

Be still.
The whole day is yours.

Enjoy cocktails at 5 P.M.

It's always 5 P.M. somewhere.

Go where there's no such thing as snow.

You've prepared for tomorrow.
Now tomorrow is here.
Relax.
Enjoy.

**Don't think of it as sagging—
think of it as "hanging out."**

THERE ARE ALWAYS NEW ROADS TO TRAVEL

It's never too late
to get your groove back.

You just have to remember
where you left it.

Now you can do things
working people can't do.

Like laugh that Monday's coming.

There are many kinds of gardens
to grow—many kinds of seeds to
plant.

Getting older is something
you never become an expert in,
no matter how long you do it.

If everyone knew how good
retirement could be,
they wouldn't waste
so much time working.

There is one constant in life:

there still won't be time to get
everything done.

**Don't' worry, you are not getting slower.
It's just that everyone else is moving faster.**

It's not a retirement so much as a 52-week paid vacation.

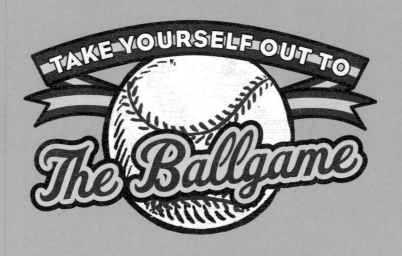